Action for the Environment

Saving Wildlife

Rufus Bellamy

FRANKLIN WATTS

This edition 2006

Franklin Watts
338 Euston Road
London NW1 3BH

Franklin Watts Australia
Hachette Children's Books
Level 17/207 Kent Street
Sydney, NSW 2000

© 2004 Franklin Watts
ISBN-10: 0-7496-6949-7
ISBN-13: 978-0-7496-6949-2

Dewey Classification: 333.95'416

A CIP catalogue record for this book
is available from the British Library

Printed in Malaysia

Editor: Adrian Cole
Design: Proof Books
Art Direction: Jonathan Hair
Picture Research: Kathy Lockley

Acknowledgements
ACO Wildlife, a division of ACO Technologies plc 18 b.
Animals Asia Foundation/www.animalsasia.org 23 b. ARS,
USDA/Photo by Keith Weller 6/Photo by Scott Bauer 21 b. Jon
Bower/Ecoscene 20. Mike Brossley/WDCS 5. Mark
Carwardine/Still Pictures COVER tr, 27. Manfred
Danegger/N.H.P.A. COVER tl. Nigel J. Dennis/N.H.P.A. 28. ©
Digital Vision Ltd. All rights reserved 14, 16, 22. Ron
Giling/Still Pictures 11. Greenpeace/Eric Algra 17 b, /Gavin
Newman 21 t. © Stichting Greenpeace Council 21 tl. Martin
Harvey/Still Pictures 19 t, 23 t. Martin Harvey/N.H.P.A. 13 t,
25 t. Hellio & Van Ingen/N.H.P.A. 19 b. ITDG/Jon Hellin 17 t.
Frans Lemmens/Still Pictures 9. David Lucas 4. Eero
Murtomaki/N.H.P.A. 7 b. Gilles Nicolet/Still Pictures 2, 12.
Robert Pickett/Ecoscene 25 b. Heinz Plenge/Still Pictures 1, 8.
Alain Pons/Still Pictures COVER b, 13 b. Rex Features 24. Ray
Roberts/Ecoscene 29. © Save-the-Rhino 7 t, 31. Michael
Sewell/Still Pictures 15. © Alan Watson/Forest Light 10. WWF-
Canon/Susan A. MAINKA 26.-

Contents

Wildlife in danger

There are millions of different types – or species – of plants and animals in the world. Some of these species are threatened or endangered because they exist in such small numbers that they could easily die out altogether and become extinct.

EXTINCTION IS FOR EVER

Many species have already become extinct. For example, some scientists believe dinosaurs became extinct because of severe changes in the Earth's climate. Today, many animals face extinction because people hunt them, or destroy the places where they live – their habitats. This has happened to the tiger: less than 3,000–4,000 tigers now remain in the wild – between 3–8% of the number that existed in the 1900s.

A young gorilla. Gorillas are one of the most endangered animals in the world. If more is not done to protect them in the wild they could soon only exist in zoos.

SAVING WILDLIFE AROUND THE WORLD

All over the world people are working to protect plants and animals. There are many projects that effectively protect endangered wildlife and allow plants and animals to reproduce successfully. Unfortunately, many species remain in danger and there is a lot of work left to do.

The Australian Whale and Dolphin Conservation Society runs an adopt-a-dolphin scheme in which people can fund the protection of dolphins such as these. People who take part get a picture of 'their' dolphin.

Action stations

The Bottlenose Dolphins that swim in the Port River, near Adelaide in Australia, face many hazards. These include motorboats, rubbish and pollution. To help save these animals laws are being passed to create a sanctuary that will hopefully protect them. However, campaigners, including the Whale and Dolphin Conservation Society, say that even stronger laws are needed to ensure a safe future for these intelligent animals.

Why protect species?

All living things – including humans – depend on other animals and plants to survive. It is therefore important to give all species as much protection as possible – even ugly-looking insects!

FOOD WEBS

Plants and animals are linked together in food chains or webs. If one species is lost, then the species that are linked to it suffer. For example, if farm chemicals kill the flowers and insects in a field, there is less food for birds. Bird numbers can therefore drop. If a species becomes extinct, the impact on other species can be devastating.

Unfortunately, many human activities, such as modern farming, reduce the number of different species in a particular area.

SAVE THE ...

Many campaigns to save wildlife focus on one particular species, such as the rhinoceros, whale or elephant. These animals attract a lot of public interest and people are willing to give money to help them. This money is often used to protect the habitats these animals live in, which also helps the other species that live there.

These runners in Europe have dressed up to raise money for Save the Rhino International.

Action stations

The White-tailed Sea Eagle lives near water in the Baltic region of Europe where it hunts for fish. In the 1970s, man-made chemical pollutants (mainly from farming and manufacturing) poisoned the fish. The eagles ate the fish, became poisoned themselves and stopped having as many young. Most of the damaging pollutants have now been banned and the WWF has provided the eagles with non-toxic food and protected nest sites. As a result, the number of White-tailed Sea Eagles in the area is rising slowly.

The plight of the White-tailed Sea Eagle shows how different species are dependent on each other. It also shows that most living things need a clean and healthy environment in order to survive.

Safe havens

The biggest threat to wildlife is the destruction of the places where plants grow and animals live. For example, Giant Pandas are endangered because over half of the bamboo forests that they depend on have been lost.

SURVIVAL SPACES

In many countries plants and animals are conserved in special protected areas. These areas range in size from small nature reserves to enormous national parks. In Peru, the Tambopata Reserve covers over 1.5 million hectares. It is home to tens of thousands of species of plants and animals including rare orchids, giant otters, anacondas and jaguars.

The Tambopata Reserve is home to the rare jaguar. Despite being protected, the reserve is still threatened by human activity.

DO NOT DISTURB

Tourists visit many protected areas to see the
wildlife. It is important that visitors do not disturb
the plants or animals they see, so most parks
have strict rules. In the Great Barrier Reef Marine
Park in Australia, divers are not allowed to take
any coral or damage the reef with boat anchors.
New eco-working holidays are also organised in
many countries, during which visitors can take
part in conservation work.

Action stations

The Kruger National Park in South
Africa is home to five of the most
well-known animals in Africa:
lions, elephants, leopards, buffalo and
rhinoceros. Elephants breed so successfully in
the park that they have had to be culled in the
past, because there was not enough room for
them all. Park staff are now experimenting with
ways to stop the elephants breeding so quickly.

*An elephant
crossing a road in
the Kruger
National Park. To
help deal with
increasing numbers
of elephants the
park is being
linked with other
protected areas.*

Helping habitats

Habitats around the world are under threat from pressures such as building, logging, pollution and farming. Problems even affect many protected areas where people kill animals and harvest plants illegally.

RESTORING HABITATS

In many places where plant and animal habitats have been destroyed, people are working to restore or recreate what has been lost. In Scotland a group of volunteers called Trees for Life is replanting hundreds of thousands of Scots pines. They want to restore part of the ancient Caledonian Forest that used to cover much of the Highlands.

This volunteer in Scotland is planting trees to help restore the country's wildlife.

SOWING SEEDS FOR THE FUTURE

Modern farming is a major threat to many species because it destroys important habitats, such as wildflower meadows. Now, however, an increasing number of environmentally-aware farmers and other groups are planting trees and hedges, and sowing wildflower seeds. This will encourage birds, insects and other wildlife back into the countryside.

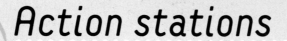

Action stations

One of the biggest causes of species loss is the destruction of tropical rainforests for timber or agricultural land. But in parts of the Amazon rainforest in Brazil, people are using the forest in a way that does not endanger the plants and animals it contains. They collect and sell products like Brazil nuts and medicinal oils that can be harvested from the forest without chopping it down.

Harvesting edible roots from the rainforest. People can use the forest without endangering wildlife.

Stop the killing

Many animals are hunted or trapped for their meat, skin, fur or other parts. For example, rhinoceros are hunted for their horns which are turned into powder and used in medicines. This killing has forced many animals to the brink of extinction.

Teachers take a group of school children on a tour of the Korup rainforest in Cameroon. Education projects, such as this one, help to stop children becoming the collectors and poachers of the future.

COLLECTORS AND POACHERS

In many countries there are laws to stop people collecting or poaching endangered wildlife. The collection and hunting of other less-threatened plants and animals is also carefully controlled so that they do not become endangered. Unfortunately, poverty and greed still drive people to make money by collecting plants and killing animals illegally.

GUARDS AND EDUCATION

To stop plants and animals being killed, many nature reserves employ guards. They work to protect wildlife from poachers who are often armed. However, guards cannot protect all wildlife. Education projects offer another solution. They can help people to understand why wildlife is important and encourage them to get involved in conservation.

In many countries poaching is bringing some species close to extinction, despite the best efforts of wildlife wardens and guards.

Action stations

Tigers are a protected species; however, medicines made from tiger bones can be sold for a lot of money. As a result tigers are hunted illegally. In India, guards protect the main national parks where many tigers live. To provide a longer-term solution in these parks, 'eco-tourism projects' have also been set up that benefit local people. This makes it more likely that they will help conserve the tigers rather than hunt them.

Corbett National Park in India is home to many tigers, like this one, and is protected by guards. However, even here, poachers still manage to kill these magnificent animals.

Stop the trade

One way to save endangered plants and animals is to stop people buying and selling them, or products made from them. If this happens there will be no money to be made from illegal hunting or plant collecting.

BANNING THE TRADE

CITES (The Convention on International Trade in Endangered Species of Wild Fauna and Flora) is a major international law that bans worldwide trade in over 800 species of endangered animal, such as whales and rhinoceros, and plants, such as rare orchids. Every year police and customs officers, with the help of environmental investigators, arrest people for smuggling banned wildlife products and stop people selling them.

Elephant tusks seized in Africa. Through the hard work of customs officers and investigators, many ivory smugglers are caught and put out of business.

CHANGING TRADITIONS

Educating people is another way the trade in endangered species can be stopped. Many animals are killed because parts of them are used in traditional medicine. This happens in places such as southeast Asia. Now, conservation groups are working in countries such as Singapore to show people that alternatives do exist.

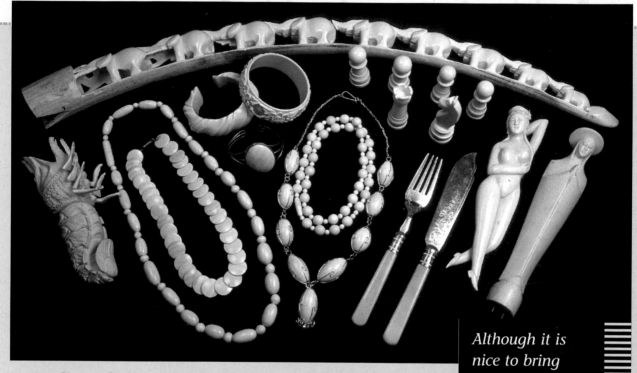

Action stations

When you are on holiday, you can help to reduce the trade in endangered wildlife. Do not buy things such as shells and coral, or anything made from animal parts. In some holiday resorts you can get your photograph taken with a bear or chimpanzee — these animals have often been illegally captured in the wild, so try not to support this activity.

Although it is nice to bring back a souvenir, do not choose endangered animal products, such as these made with ivory. Instead choose something that supports local conservation efforts.

Marine matters

Many fish and other sea creatures are threatened because too many have been caught by large fishing fleets around the world. Species that used to be plentiful, such as cod, have dropped in number significantly.

FISHING ACTION

Fish are a vital source of food for many people. Yet, around 70% of the world's fish stocks are overfished. Many countries, such as those in the European Union, are trying to conserve fish stocks by reducing the size of their fishing fleets. To reduce the impact on other wildlife, such as dolphins, laws have also been introduced to limit the size and type of nets used by fishing boats and the number and type of fish they can catch.

Fishing can harm many marine animals, including dolphins such as this one, which get caught in the nets of some fishermen.

MARINE RESERVES

In many countries conservation groups are working with local people to set up fishery reserves. In these protected areas fish can breed safely – raising fish stock numbers. The Intermediate Technology Development Group is helping several communities in Bangladesh and India.

This pond is part of an ITDG project that aims to 'grow' more fish. It is a vital community food source.

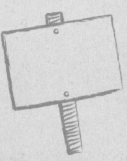

Action stations

Blue Whales are the largest creatures in the ocean, growing up to 30 metres long and weighing about 150,000 kilograms. Many whale species, including Blue Whales, are endangered and a lot has been done to protect them – there is a ban on commercial whaling, and a whale sanctuary has been set up in the seas around Antarctica. Despite this, many whale species are threatened because they are killed illegally or their feeding grounds are disrupted or polluted. Organisations, such as Greenpeace, campaign to save whales.

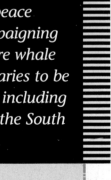

Greenpeace is campaigning for more whale sanctuaries to be set up, including one in the South Pacific.

A helping hand

Many of the things that people do, such as building roads and houses, seriously affect or kill plants and animals. However, there is a lot we can do to help the wildlife that lives around us.

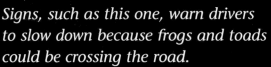
Signs, such as this one, warn drivers to slow down because frogs and toads could be crossing the road.

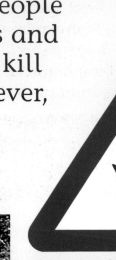

GETTING AROUND SAFELY

Busy places, such as roads, are dangerous and stop animals moving around safely. Some roads now have small tunnels underneath them to help animals, such as toads, cross without getting run over. Other barriers, such as walls, can have small gaps built into them. Man-made dams in rivers can have special channels to allow fish, such as salmon, to swim upriver to breed.

Tunnels such as this one help wildlife, including toads and small animals, cross roads in safety.

SOMEWHERE TO LIVE AND BREED

Many animals, particularly in cities, cannot easily find a place to live and breed. To help, many people and conservation groups put up bird, bat or bug boxes, or even erect special 'tree houses' for owls to live in. Many animals only need peace and quiet. In Turkey, special beaches are set aside in some busy tourist areas so that turtles can lay their eggs undisturbed.

Sea turtles need safe beaches on which to nest, because, when they hatch, baby turtles burrow out of the sand and head towards the sea.

Action stations

If you have a garden at home or at school then you can help to give animals a place to live and something to eat. Put out food and water for the birds that visit, and put up a bird box. Sow an area of wildflowers to attract insects and create a log pile in the shade to provide them with shelter.

This young girl is helping to feed birds in a public park. Parks are often good places to see lots of wildlife, such as rabbits and squirrels.

Pollution clean-up

Human waste, rubbish and other pollution harm and kill plants and animals around the world. Many are poisoned by waste spills or are suffocated by rubbish. But people are campaigning to save wildlife by putting a stop to pollution.

CHEMICAL SOUP

Animals such as fish, alligators and polar bears have been found with cancer and other health problems that are thought to have been caused by some man-made chemical pollutants. Among the worst of these are Persistent Organic Pollutants (POPs), which can travel long distances in the air. Now groups, such as Greenpeace and the WWF, are calling on governments to pass stricter laws controlling these and other polluting chemicals.

Marine litter is just one type of pollution that affects animals. It is estimated over 1 million birds die each year because they eat or are tangled in plastic rubbish. Many groups work to clean up areas to stop this happening.

SAVE OUR CLIMATE

Action stations

One of the most worrying environmental problems is global warming. Many scientists believe it is caused by 'greenhouse' gases, such as carbon dioxide, produced mainly by cars and power stations. The Earth could warm up by a few degrees Celsius in the next 100 years, threatening thousands of species with extinction. Greenpeace is running the 'Save Our Climate' campaign so that everyone can help to solve the problem.

GOING ORGANIC

Farm chemicals have caused a big drop in the number of insect and plant species in the countryside. To try and help wildlife, organic farmers have stopped using artificial chemicals completely. Organic farmers encourage insects that eat pests to come into their fields. These friendly bugs include ladybirds and lacewing larvae.

A ladybird can eat 5,000 aphids in its lifetime.

Animal rescue

Habitat destruction, pollution and other man-made problems harm countless animals. In many countries, dedicated teams of people work to rescue and save as many injured animals as possible.

When animals, such as this orang-utan, have been nursed back to health at the Wanariset sanctuary, they are released back into protected forest areas.

ORANG-UTAN HOSPITAL

Around the world, forest fires drive millions of animals from their homes. In Indonesia this is an especially big problem and there are a number of sanctuaries that treat and care for injured forest animals. At the Wanariset Centre in Kalimantan, for example, orang-utans that have been made homeless are treated for any injuries or illnesses.

BIRD CLEAN-UP

Oil spills poison many marine animals each year. One of the worst was the Exxon Valdez disaster in 1989 in which millions of gallons of crude oil polluted water in Prince William Sound in Alaska, USA. Although many thousands of otters and birds died, animal experts and volunteers were able to clean up and save some animals.

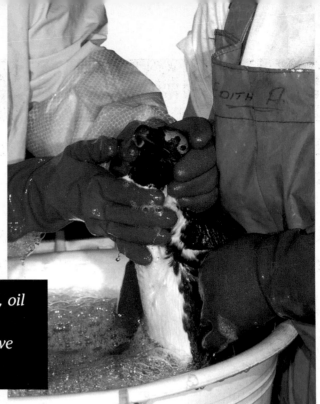

Despite the Exxon Valdez tragedy, oil spills still happen today and volunteers still have to try and save the marine creatures affected.

Action stations

In China, some people use the bile produced by the gall bladders of Moon Bears as a medicine. These bears are kept in cruel conditions in cages. To save these bears a group called the Animals Asia Foundation has worked to free the animals and treat them in a special sanctuary where they are nursed back to health. So far the foundation has rescued hundreds of bears.

Moon Bear rescue. The work of the Animals Asia Foundation (see www.animalsasia.org) also involves convincing people to use alternative medicines to the Moon Bear bile.

A last chance?

Most large zoos do more than simply display animals. Many of them have programmes for captive breeding and reintroducing rare animals back into the wild. Many botanical gardens collect, store and grow rare plant varieties so that they are not lost for ever.

CAPTIVE BREEDING

One of the leading centres for captive breeding in the world is Jersey Zoo in the Channel Islands. This zoo – which was set up by Gerald Durrell – breeds many endangered animals, such as the Ring-tailed Lemur and the Aye-aye. San Diego Zoo's Wild Animal Park in the USA also runs breeding programmes. For example, it has helped to increase the California Condor population from 25 in 1983 to 242 in June 2004. Captive breeding makes sure that even if a species dies out in the wild, it does not become extinct.

Jersey Zoo has helped run a captive breeding programme for the Echo Parakeet in the bird's native home, the island of Mauritius. The zoo also runs an education programme to teach people about the threats facing this bird and many other endangered animals.

REINTRODUCTION

The aim of captive breeding in many zoos is to reintroduce animals into the wild. For example in Australia, the Tasmanian National Parks and Wildlife Service has been running a project to reintroduce the Orange-bellied Parrot. There are only a few hundred of these birds left in the wild.

This baby parrot is being hand-fed. The only way to save some endangered species is to breed them in controlled conditions, where they can grow in safety. When this bird is old enough it will be released into the wild.

Action stations

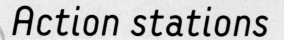

The Golden Lion Tamarin is threatened by the destruction of its home in the coastal forests of Brazil. Pockets of forest have been protected and over 100 zoos around the world have worked together to breed the Golden Lion Tamarin in captivity. In recent years, over 140 animals have been released into the wild. This strategy seems to be working: the Golden Lion Tamarin population in the wild has risen from around 200 to more than 1,000.

The Golden Lion Tamarin is found only in lowland coastal forests of Brazil.

Panda protection

The Giant Panda is the symbol of the world's largest independent conservation organisation – the WWF. The protection and conservation of the Giant Panda highlights many of the main issues that affect almost all endangered species.

PANDAS IN PERIL

There are now only about 1,600 Giant Pandas in the wild. Giant Pandas are threatened by the same problems that affect almost all endangered wildlife: habitat destruction and poaching. Their forest homes in the mountain regions of southwest China have been heavily logged and cleared for farming. Now, many Giant Pandas live in small areas of bamboo vegetation little more than a kilometre wide.

Giant Pandas are threatened by the loss of bamboo forests and by poaching. This Giant Panda cub was rescued after its mother was killed.

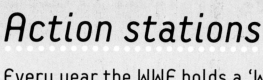

Action stations

Every year the WWF holds a 'Walk for Wildlife'. In 2001 (WWF's 40th birthday) it raised money for Giant Panda projects in China. The group – the first international conservation organisation to work in China – used the money to fund research, training, education and the practical management of Giant Panda reserves.

Vets in China examine a Giant Panda as part of a captive breeding programme. The WWF has many projects that help protect Giant Pandas.

HABITAT HELP

To protect Giant Pandas the Chinese government has created a number of protected reserves and has banned logging in some areas where Giant Pandas live. However, Giant Pandas are still killed illegally and more needs to be done to save them. One proposal is the development of more 'bamboo corridors' to link areas where Giant Pandas live so that they can move around to eat and breed more easily.

People and wildlife

Almost everything we do has some effect on the plants and animals around us. One of the greatest challenges we face is to find ways of sharing the planet with the wildlife that lives here.

ENVIRONMENTALLY-FRIENDLY PEOPLE

In many countries people are becoming more aware of the environment. They are starting to change the way they do things, such as travelling, shopping and working so that they have less environmental impact. Some far-sighted companies are also striving to become environmentally-friendly by reducing the effect their factories and products have on wildlife.

In Madagascar, local people are training as wildlife guides to show tourists their country's endangered wildlife.

Action stations

One of the best ways to get involved and help to save wildlife is by joining an organisation, such as the WWF. If you are interested in one particular animal – such as the dolphin – you will almost certainly be able to join a specific group. As a member you will be able to help the group raise money and get involved in its work.

These volunteers are hard at work clearing rubbish from a towpath along a canal – an important man-made habitat for water birds and other animals.

PROTECTING BIODIVERSITY

Many governments are helping people to save wildlife by creating laws and initiatives that protect areas where endangered plants and animals grow and live. Some action plans aim to conserve the number of species living in a particular area – its biodiversity. But plans like these will only work if everyone plays their part. If we do not, the world will lose many more wonderful plants and animals.

Glossary

Biodiversity The variety of different species of living things that exist in a given area.

Botanical garden A place where a large number of different species of plants are grown. Botanical gardens are often open to the public.

Carbon dioxide The main greenhouse gas. Carbon dioxide occurs naturally, but is also produced when fossil fuels, such as oil, coal and gas, are burnt.

Coral A marine creature that lives in warm seas. Coral has a skeleton of calcium carbonate (lime). As coral dies, these skeletons gradually form reefs that are home to a variety of marine wildlife.

Eco-tourism A type of holiday designed so that visitors have as little environmental impact as possible on the places they visit.

Environmentally-friendly A product or activity that has as little environmental impact as possible, or which helps protect, restore or conserve the environment.

Extinction The complete disappearance of a species from the planet.

Food chain or web The feeding relationships that exist between the different species of animals and plants that live in a certain area.

Gall bladder A small sac that is part of the digestive system. The gall bladder stores bile from the liver, where it is produced as part of the digestive process.

Global warming The gradual rise in the Earth's temperature.

Greenhouse gases The gases that are thought by many scientists to be causing global warming. The main ones are carbon dioxide and methane.

Habitat The place where a plant or animal lives.

Organic Organic farming uses no man-made chemicals. Instead, natural products such as animal waste are used to make crops grow stronger.

Poacher A person who hunts, traps or kills an animal illegally.

POPs Longlasting, hazardous chemicals that were used in a number of industrial processes and which can be produced when rubbish is burnt.

Reintroduction The process in which a species of plant or animal is put back into a habitat from which it has disappeared.

Species A group of plants or animals that are very similar to each other and can reproduce together.

Tropical rainforest A type of forest that is usually found near the equator where it is hot and wet.

WWF One of the world's leading environmental groups that campaigns for the protection of wildlife and the natural environment.

Zoo A place where animals are kept in captivity for the public to look at. Many carry out breeding programmes and conservation awareness-raising programmes.

Find out more

www.btcv.org

The website of the UK's leading practical conservation charity. Find out what people can do to create, restore and protect wildlife habitats.

www.cites.org

Find out all about CITES and take a look at the species database to see which animals are endangered.

www.durrellwildlife.org

Find out all about Durrell Wildlife's mission to save wild animals from extinction. Click on the link to the Jersey Zoo to find out all about captive breeding programmes.

www.greenpeace.org

Visit this site to find out about Greenpeace and its campaigns to conserve wildlife and the habitats in which it lives.

www.itdg.org

Website of 'Practical Action' (formerly called the ITDG). Features information about projects in the developing world that are helping people escape from poverty, so they can look after the environment more easily.

www.panda.org

The WWF's website contains an amazing range of information about endangered species. Click on the 'flagship species' link to find out what is being done to conserve the world's rarest animals.

www.wdcs.org

Find out all about the protection of whales and dolphins at the site of the world's most active charity dedicated to their conservation and welfare.

Index